Bodleian Library
Souvenir Guide

Geoffrey Tyack

Contents

Introduction

Oxford's libraries are among the most celebrated in
the world, not only for their incomparable collections
of books and manuscripts, but also for their buildings,
some of which have remained in continuous use since
the Middle Ages. Among them the Bodleian, the chief
among the University's libraries, has a special place.
First opened to scholars in 1602, it incorporates an
earlier library erected by the University in the fifteenth
century to house books donated by Humfrey, Duke of
Gloucester. Since 1602 it has expanded, slowly at first
but with increasing momentum over the last 150 years,
to keep pace with the ever-growing accumulation of
books and papers, but the core of the old buildings
remains intact. These buildings are still used by students
and scholars from all over the world, and they attract an
ever-increasing number of visitors, for whose benefit this
guide has been written.

Duke Humfrey's Library (right). The north elevation of the Divinity
School (previous page).

4

History

The first library for Oxford University – as distinct from the colleges – was housed in a room above the Old Congregation House, begun c.1320 on a site to the north of the chancel of the University Church of St Mary the Virgin. The building stood at the heart of Oxford's 'academic quarter', close to the schools in which lectures were given. The library was built with funds supplied by Thomas de Cobham, Bishop of Worcester, but was still unfinished when he died in 1327. The room, which still exists as a meeting room for the church, is neither large nor architecturally impressive, and it was superseded in 1488 by the library known as Duke Humfrey's, which constitutes the oldest part of the Bodleian complex. The occasion for moving to a new building was the gift to the University by Humfrey, Duke of Gloucester, younger brother of King Henry V, of his priceless collection of more than 281 manuscripts, including several important classical texts. These volumes would have made the existing library desperately over crowded, and in 1444 the University decided to erect a new library over the Divinity School, begun in about 1424 on a site at the northern end of School Street, just inside the town wall. Because of chronic shortages of funds the building was still unfinished in the 1440s, and the library was not begun in earnest until 1478; it was finally opened ten years later.

Duke Humfrey's library survived in its original form for just over sixty years; in 1550 it was denuded of its books after a visitation by Richard Cox, Dean of the newly founded Christ Church. He was acting under legislation passed by King Edward VI designed to purge the English church of all traces of Roman Catholicism, including 'superstitious books and images'. In the words of the historian Anthony Wood, 'some of those books so taken out by the Reformers were burnt, some sold away for Robin Hood's pennyworths, either to Booksellers, or to Glovers to press their gloves, or Taylors to make measures, or to Bookbinders to cover books bound by them, and some also kept by the Reformers for their own use'. Oxford University was not a wealthy institution and did not have the resources to build up a collection of new printed books to replace those dispersed. Therefore, in 1556 the desks were sold, and the room was taken over by the Faculty of Medicine.

The library was rescued by Sir Thomas Bodley (1545–1613), a Fellow of Merton College who had travelled extensively in Europe and had, between 1585 and 1596, carried out several diplomatic missions for Queen Elizabeth I. He married a rich widow whose husband had made a fortune from trading in pilchards and, in his retirement from public life, decided, in his

Sir Thomas Bodley

own words, to 'set up my staff at the library door in Oxon; being thoroughly persuaded, that in my solitude, and surcease from the Commonwealth affairs, I could not busy myself to better purpose, than by reducing that place (which then in every part lay ruined and waste) to the public use of students'. His money was accepted in 1598, and the old library was refurnished to house a new collection of some 2,500 books, some of them given by Bodley himself, some by other donors. A librarian, Thomas James, was appointed, and the library finally opened on 8 November 1602. The first printed catalogue followed in 1605; a new edition of 1620 ran to 675 pages.

In 1610 Bodley entered into an agreement with the Stationers' Company of London under which a copy of every book published in England and registered at Stationers' Hall would be deposited in the new library. Although at first the agreement was honoured more in the breach than in the observance, it nevertheless pointed to the future of the library as a comprehensive and ever-expanding collection, different in both size and purpose from the libraries of the colleges. More immediately it imposed an extra strain on space within the building, which was already housing many more books than originally foreseen; new gifts of books made the lack of space ever more acute. So in 1610–12 Bodley planned and financed the first extension to the medieval building, known as Arts End.

Bodley died in 1613 and, on the day after his funeral, work started on the building of a spacious quadrangle of buildings (the Schools Quadrangle) to the east of the library. Bodley was the prime mover in this ambitious project, but most of the money was raised by loans and public subscription. The buildings were designed to house lecture and examination rooms ('schools' in Oxford parlance) to replace what Bodley called 'those ruinous little rooms' on the site in which generations of undergraduates had been taught. In his will Bodley left money to add a third floor designed to serve as 'a very large supplement for stowage of books', which also became a public museum and picture gallery, the first in England. The quadrangle was structurally complete by 1619, but work on fitting it out continued until at least 1624.

The last addition to Bodley's buildings came in 1634–7, when another extension to Duke Humfrey's library was built; still known as Selden End, after the lawyer John Selden (1584–1654) who made a gift of 8,000 books which were housed there, it stands at the far end of the Divinity School, over the Convocation House, the meeting-room for the University's 'Parliament'. The library was now able to receive and house numerous gifts of books and, especially, manuscripts: from the 3rd Earl of Pembroke in 1629, from Sir Kenelm Digby in 1634, from William Laud, Archbishop of Canterbury, starting in 1635, and from many others. It was the collections of manuscripts, as much as those of books, which attracted scholars from all over Europe, irrespective of whether or not they were members of the University of Oxford, a tradition

Three early benefactors: Archbishop William Laud (above left), Sir Kenelm Digby (below left), John Selden (bottom right). Charles I attempted unsuccessfully to borrow a book from the Bodleian (above right).

which the Bodleian still keeps up (undergraduates, on the other hand, were rarely admitted until quite recent times). Another tradition, still zealously guarded, is that no books were to be lent to readers; even King Charles I was refused permission to borrow a book in 1645. But the number of users should not be overestimated; in 1831 there was an average of three or four readers a day, and there were no readers at all in July. With no heating until 1845 and no artificial lighting until 1929, the Library only opened from 10am to 3pm in the winter and 9am to 4pm in the summer.

The growth of the collection slowed down in the early eighteenth century when the library, like the University as a whole, entered into a somewhat somnolent period; no books at all were purchased between 1700 and 1703. Yet the late seventeenth and early eighteenth centuries saw a spate of library-building in Oxford. Most of the new libraries were built by the colleges, but the finest of all, at least from an architectural point of view, was the brainchild of an individual, Dr John Radcliffe (1650–1714), perhaps the most successful English physician of his day. He left his trustees a large sum of money with which to purchase both the land for the new building and an endowment to pay a librarian and purchase books. The site eventually chosen was to the south of the Schools Quadrangle, in the middle of a new square (Radcliffe Square) formed by the demolition of old houses in School Street and Catte Street and bounded by All Souls and Brasenose Colleges and the University Church. Here, between

The façade of Arts End in the Old Schools Quadrangle.

1737 and 1748, the monumental circular domed building – Oxford's most impressive piece of classical architecture – went up to the designs of James Gibbs, and it was finally opened in 1749.

For many years the Radcliffe Library, as it was called until 1860, was something of a white elephant. It was completely independent of the Bodleian, readers were few in number, the heterogeneous collection of books served no obvious purpose, and the first librarians displayed a strange reluctance to add to it. Matters improved in the early nineteenth century, when a collection of books on medicine and natural history was gradually amassed: something celebrated by the publication of the first printed catalogue in 1835. Meanwhile the Bodleian's collections had begun to grow again. Successive pieces of legislation made the agreement with the Stationers' Company more effective, so that by 1842 the library could concentrate its purchases on manuscripts and foreign books, secure in the knowledge that new books published in England would be deposited free of charge. Gifts of books and manuscripts continued to be made, notably that of 18,000 printed books (including 300 incunabula – books printed before 1500) and 393 manuscripts from the bequest of Francis Douce in 1834. In 1849, six years after the publication of a new catalogue in three folio volumes, there were estimated to be 220,000 books and some 21,000 manuscripts in the library's collection.

The Bodleian was not only a collection of books and manuscripts; it also housed pictures, sculptures, coins and medals, and 'curiosities': objects of scientific, exotic or historical interest, including even a stuffed crocodile

from Jamaica. Old pictures show these eclectic collections in different parts of the present library buildings, but especially in the gallery on the top floor of the Schools Quadrangle. In 1755 the collections were augmented by the Countess of Pomfret's gift of a large part of the Arundel Marbles, the first collection of antique statuary to be formed in England. They were housed in two of the ground-floor rooms around the quadrangle no longer needed for teaching. Starting in 1788, the rooms on the first floor were given over to library use, including the storage of manuscripts, and with the opening of the University Galleries – now the Ashmolean Museum – in Beaumont Street in 1845 the marbles were transferred to a more suitable setting, as were seventy pictures from the top-floor gallery. This left more space for storing books, which was further increased in 1859 when the University agreed to relinquish the last of its ground-floor lecture rooms; they were rehoused in 1876–82 in the new Examination Schools in the High Street. With its completion the whole of the Schools Quadrangle was at last in the hands of the library, save for two rooms in the tower in which the Oxford University archives were kept.

A further increase in space came about in 1860, when the Radcliffe Library was taken over by the Bodleian and renamed the Radcliffe Camera (the word camera means 'room' in Latin). The upper-floor library became a reading-room, used mainly by undergraduates, who had been admitted to the Bodleian since 1856, and the ground floor was turned into a book-stack (it was converted into a second reading room in 1941). Thus the library acquired its first major addition of space for readers since the building of Selden End in 1634; by the beginning of the twentieth century an average of a hundred people a day were using it. The medical and scientific books formerly kept in the Radcliffe Camera were moved to new premises in the University Museum in South Parks Road; they were later transferred to the adjacent but much larger Radcliffe Science Library, built to the designs of Thomas Graham Jackson, architect of the Examination Schools, in 1897–1901.

By the end of the nineteenth century, the Bodleian's book collection was growing by more than 30,000 volumes a year, and the number of books had reached the million mark by 1914. To provide extra storage space an underground book store was excavated beneath Radcliffe Square in 1909–12; at the time it was the largest such store in the world, and the first to use modern compact shelving. But with both readers and books inexorably increasing the pressure on space once more became critical, leading some members of the University to propose moving the library to a more spacious site elsewhere, as was done in Cambridge when its new University Library was built in 1931–4. This did not happen, however, and in 1931 the decision was taken to build a new library, housing book-stacks for five million books, library departments and reading rooms, on a site occupied by a row of old timber houses on the north side of Broad Street. The new building went up to the designs of Sir Giles Gilbert Scott, architect of the Cambridge University Library, in 1937–40.

The building of the New Library allowed some rationalization of the older buildings to allow more space

The Radcliffe Camera.

12

for the growing numbers of undergraduates, graduate students and visiting scholars. The former gallery on the top floor of the Schools Quadrangle had already become a reading room (the Upper Reading Room), and the former schools on the floor below, long used for book-storage, now became the Lower Reading Room, leaving the ground floor for offices. In 1960–3 Duke Humfrey's library underwent a major restoration, including the refacing of its decaying, blackened façades in Clipsham stone, along with those of Selden End and Arts End; the refacing of the rest of the Schools Quadrangle followed in 1964–8. In 1975 new office space was acquired in the Clarendon Building, built for the University Press in 1712–13, and occupying the crucial site between the Old and New Libraries. Thus the whole area between the Radcliffe Camera and the New Library – the historic core of the University – came into the hands of the Bodleian.

A thirteenth-century English Manuscript of the Apocalypse (left) and a printed copy of Pliny's *Natural History* illuminated by hand, both from the bequest of Francis Douce.

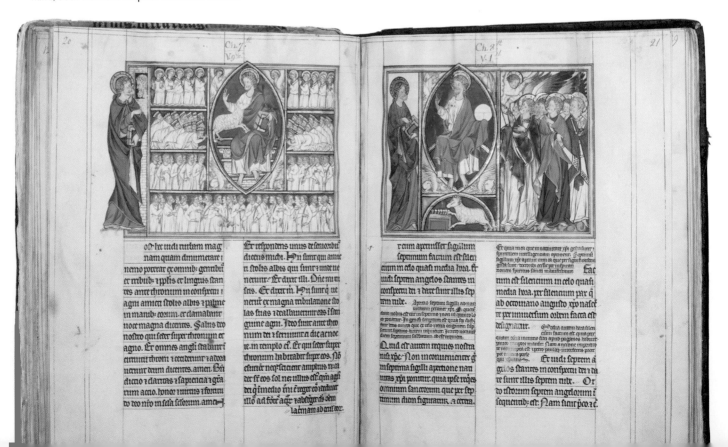

LIBRO PRIMO DELLA NATVRALE HISTORIA DI. C. PLINIO SECONDO TRADOCTA IN LINGVA FIOREN TINA PER CHRISTOPHORO LANDINO FIORENTI NO ALSERENISSIMO FERDINANDO RE DI NAPOLI.

PREFATIONE

ITERMINAI O GIOCONDISSIMO imperadore con epistola forse di troppa licétia narrarti elibri della historia naturale: opera no uella alle muse romane: nata apresso di me nel lultima genitura. Sia adunq; questa prefatiõe uerissima di te métre che gia inuecchia nel grã dissimo tuo padre: per che usando el uerso di Catullo mio compatriota tu soleui pure stima re qualche chosa le mie ciácie. Tu conosci que sta castrense & militare parola. Et lui chome tu sai mutando le prime syllabe si fece alquanto piu duro che non uolea essere stimato da tuoi familiari & serui. Per questo adunq; ditermi nai scriuerti: & áchora per che le nostre chose apparischino & sieno manifeste p questa mia audacia maxime doléndoti tu che pel passato non lhabbi facto in una altra nostra procace epistola. Et accio che tutti glhuomini sappino quanto di pari lomperio techo uiua: Tu elquale hai triomphato & se stato censore & sei uolte cósolo & participe del la tribunitia potesta: Se stato prefecto del pretorio: ilche hai facto piu nobile che tutti glaltri magistrati: perche per piacere a tuo padre & allordine equestre lacceptasti: Et tutte queste cose per rispecto della republica hai facto: Et me chome nel contubernio castrense tractasti? Et certo niéte ha mutato inte lamplitudine & grandezza della tua fortuna: se non che tanto piu possi & uogla giouare: quáto quella e maggiore. Adúq; béche a tutti glaltri huomini sia aperta la uia a impetrare ogni chosa da te uenerándoti: Niente di meno solo laudacia fa che io piu familiarmente te honori. Questa audacia adunq; imputerai a te medesimo: & a te medesimo nel nostro fallo perdonerai. Io mi stroppicciai la faccia: & niente di meno nessuno proficto ho facto: perche per unaltra uia mapparisti grande: & di lontano mi rimuoui con le faccelline del tuo ingegno. Et certo in nexuno piu ffolgora quella: laquale piu ueramente e decta in te che in altri for za deloquentia. In te e quella facundia che alla tribunitia potesta si conuiene: Con qta risonantia tuoni tu le laude paterne? Cõ quanta (non sanza amore) dimostri quelle di tuo fratello? Quanto se excellente & sublime nella poetica faculta? O gran fecondita danimo. Certo hai trouato inche modo possi imitare tuo fratello. Ma queste chose chi potrebbe sanza paura considerare: hauendo a uenire al giudicio dellongegno tuo: maxime essendo quello dame prouocato? Certamente non sono in simile conditione quegli che publicano alchuno libro: & quegli che ate glintitolano. Impero che io lo publicassi & non lo intitolassi ate: potrei dire perche leggi tu queste chose o imperadore: lequali sono scripte albasso uulgo & alla turba de glagricultori & de glar tefici & a quegli che cósumano elloro otio negli studii? Perche adunq; ti fa tu giudice: concio sia che quando io scriueuo questa opera: non thaueuo posto nella tauola doue sono descripti egiudici: Et eri di tanta excellentia: che non stimauo che tu ti degnassi scendere si basso? Preterea quando bene non fussi in si excelso grado: nientedimeno gli scriptori comunemente fuggono el giudicio de docti. Questo fa Cicerone: elquale e di tanta eloquentia: che puo fare

QVOD FELICITER VORTAT
ACADEMICI OXONIENS
BIBLIOTHECAM HANC
VOBIS REIPVBLICAEQVE
LITERATORVM
T. B. P.

Architecture
The Quadrangle

The Old Library is approached through the quadrangle built to accommodate Oxford University's schools or lecture rooms. They originally took up three sides of the courtyard, with a tall gate tower on the eastern side facing Catte Street; facing it is the front of the library founded by Sir Thomas Bodley, and it is through a doorway in the centre of this range that the library is entered. Though constructed in less than ten years, from 1610 to 1619, the buildings around the quadrangle show clear signs of having been conceived and built at different times. The first part to be constructed was the façade of the library, built in 1610–12. The entrance is through a doorway in the centre, surmounted by an inscription underneath an ogee arch enclosing Bodley's coat of arms, along with that of the University.

The inscription reads: 'QUOD FELICITER VORTAT ACADEMICI OXONIENS BIBLIOTHECAM HANC VOBIS REIPUBLICAEQUE LITERATORUM T.B.P. (That it might turn out happily, Oxonian academics, for you and for the republic of lettered men Thomas Bodley placed this library)'. In front of the doorway is a bronze statue, by the French Huguenot sculptor Hubert le Sueur, of William Herbert, 3rd Earl of Pembroke, and Chancellor of Oxford University from

Entrance to the Old Library.

1617 to 1630; he donated an important collection of manuscripts to the library. The statue was moved to its present site in 1950 from the top-floor room under the tower (now part of the Upper Reading Room). The central doorway leads into the Proscholium (see below); until recent years it gave access only to the Divinity School, the library being approached by staircases that project from the two ends of the façade.

The library façade is a curiously archaic piece of architecture for its date, with Gothic 'panelling' spread over the walls, a traceried late Gothic window on the first floor and a skyline punctuated by battlements and pinnacles: features which, though common in the fifteenth and early sixteenth centuries, had largely vanished from English architecture by the early seventeenth century. This deliberate archaism proclaims Bodley's sense of continuity with the medieval past. The 'panelling' of pointed arches is copied from that of the façade of the Divinity School, as can be seen inside the Proscholium, and the battlements and pinnacles are almost identical to those of the Divinity School. The building is thus both a very late example of the survival of Gothic architecture in the legendary 'home of lost causes' and, in some respects, a precursor of the Gothic Revival.

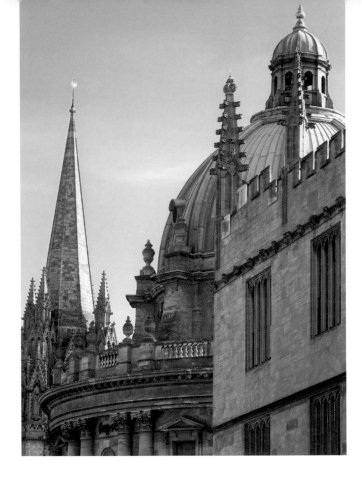

The master masons responsible for the construction of the library façade and for the early stages of the Schools Quadrangle were two men from Halifax in Yorkshire, John Akroyd and John Bentley. They came to Oxford in 1608 to build the Fellows' Quadrangle at Merton College for Bodley's friend Henry Savile, Warden of Merton and another Yorkshireman. In 1611 Bodley told the newly appointed librarian, Thomas James, that the masons would be 'so diligent and provident, as there shall be no cause for their enemies the townsmen to insult them as they did' – a reference to the animosity which their arrival caused among the Oxford masons, whose prices they undercut. But there seems little doubt that many of the important decisions about layout and architectural style were made by Bodley himself, in consultation with Savile, who continued to give advice after Bodley's death.

The remainder of the quadrangle consists of three storeys, the lower two originally occupied by the schools and the top floor by the picture gallery; the upstairs rooms were reached by staircases in rectangular projections at each of the four corners. The pointed-arched doorways gave direct access to the staircases and to the schools. These were arranged heirarchically, and their names, in Latin, are painted above the doorways, giving a graphic insight into the seventeenth-century curriculum. The more elementary subjects of the Seven Liberal Arts were placed on the east side of the quadrangle, on either side of the gate tower. On the north and south sides were the languages (Greek and Hebrew) and philosophies, with the 'higher faculties' of law and medicine closest to the library on the first floor. Theology (the 'Queen of the Sciences' in the medieval scheme of learning) remained in the Divinity School. The ground-floor rooms are now occupied by library offices, seminar rooms and a café. Vaulted passageways lead into the quadrangle from the north and south sides; the coat of arms of the University is carved over the north entrance, and that of the 3rd Earl of Pembroke over that to the south, with his family motto 'Ung je Serviray (One will I serve)' underneath; the inscription above reads: 'GUIL HERBERT PEMBROCHI COMES REGII HOSPITII CAMERARIUS HONORATISSIMUS ACADEMI CANCELLARIUS (William Herbert,

Detail of the Old Library, Radcliffe Camera, and St. Mary the Virgin (above). Entrance to one of the schools in the Old Schools Quadrangle (right).

Earl of Pembroke, Chamberlain of the Royal Household, most honoured Chancellor of the University)'.

The eastern side of the quadrangle is dominated by the five-storied gate tower known as the Tower of the Five Orders. It still retains its original oak doors to Catte Street, containing the coats of arms of the University and the colleges which were in existence in 1613, and above the round-arched entrance on the inner side is the royal coat of arms. The inner face of the tower is treated as a display of classical architectural learning: a novelty in early seventeenth-century Oxford. Twin pairs of classical columns – Tuscan, Doric, Ionic, Corinthian and Composite – are mounted one above another, each pair linked by an entablature. Such 'towers of the orders' originated in sixteenth-century France; one was also built at the centre of the south front of the Fellows' Quadrangle at Merton College, and the tower at the Bodleian is clearly influenced by it. However, although the detailing is derived from Renaissance pattern-books, the architectural framework is still Gothic. The windows are divided up by mullions and transoms in the medieval manner, and pinnacles project upwards from the four corners. The largest pinnacle, at the north-west corner contains a spiral staircase giving access to the two topmost rooms where the University's archives are kept; the top room served as a storehouse for 'powder and shot' during the Civil War and was for many years an observatory. The tower's skyline is further decorated with a display of curvaceous 'strapwork' ornament derived from

The Tower of the Five Orders.

sixteenth-century Flanders, enclosing another carving of the royal coat of arms.

Oxford's devotion to the Stuart monarchy was underlined by a decision taken in 1620, when the tower was structurally complete, to carve a statue of King James I on the fourth storey. James visited Oxford in that year and gave the University a copy of his own collected writings, an event which is symbolically represented by a figure of the King (originally painted) seated under a canopy of state on which is carved the words 'BEATI PACIFICI (Blessed are the peacemakers)'. He is presenting a book to a kneeling woman representing the University (to the right), with Fame blowing a trumpet to the left; on the books are the words 'HAEC HABEO QUAE SCRIPSI. HAEC HABEO QUAE DEDI (These things I have which I have written. These things I have which I have given)'. Underneath is a Latin inscription: 'REGNANTE D. JACOBO REGUMDOCTISSIMO MUNIFICENTISSIMO OPTIMOHAE MUSIS EXTRUCTAE MOLES.CONGESTA BIBLIOTHECA ETQUAECUNQUE ADHUC DEERANT ADSPLENDOREM ACADEMIAE FELICITERTENTATA COEPTA ABSOLUTA.SOLI DEO GLORIA (When the Lord James was reigning, most learned, most munificent, best of kings, these structures [were] built for the Muses. The library [was] put together, and whatever things were still lacking, to the splendour of the University, [were] happily attempted, begun, completed. Glory to God alone)'. The sculptor was probably John Clark, a Yorkshireman who may have been the son-in-law of the mason John Akroyd.

The quadrangle was built of limestone from Headington, two miles from Oxford. Though easy to carve, this stone did not weather well, and in 1878–84

the top floor and the gate-tower were refaced in a more durable limestone from Clipsham (Rutland) by Thomas Graham Jackson. Further remedial work in the twentieth century included the recarving of the heads which terminate the mouldings over the doorways into the schools, and in 1951–2 new portrait heads of contemporary Oxford figures (including two of Bodley's Librarians) were carved by Mark Batten on either side of the two round-arched doorways on the north and south sides. More extensive repair and refacing work was carried out, under the direction of Robert Potter, in 1964–8, again in Clipsham stone. The work encompassed the whole of the inside of the quadrangle, though some of the weathered original stonework can be seen on the outer walls.

The Great Gate (left). Detail from the Tower of the Five Orders (right).

The Proscholium and the Divinity School

Since 1968 the Bodleian Library has been entered through the Proscholium, built in 1610–12 as a vestibule to the Divinity School underneath Sir Thomas Bodley's library extension (Arts End). More a passageway than a room, the Proscholium is plainly decorated, with bare stone walls and a ribbed vault with coats of arms adorning the bosses. On the wall to the left of the entrance is a sixteenth-century portrait of William Cecil, Lord Burghley, Queen Elizabeth I's chief minister and a patron of Bodley, seated on a mule. The west wall (facing the entrance) is the lower part of the fifteenth-century façade of the Divinity School, with the blind stone 'panelling' of repeated pointed arches, which Bodley's masons copied when they built the present west front of the Schools Quadrangle, and a delicately carved doorway complete with its original wooden doors.

The Divinity School is one of the masterpieces of Late Gothic architecture, bearing comparison with anything else in fifteenth-century Europe. But the interior which we see today is by no means what was conceived when work first began on laying the foundations in 1424. The School was originally planned as a single-storied building, rather like a free-standing chapel, with a steep-pitched roof. Chronic underfunding meant that the work was constantly interrupted, and there is no evidence that the walls had even been begun until Richard Winchcombe took over as master mason in 1430. He built most of the shell of the building, including the east and west doorways and the windows with their Perpendicular tracery. But he died before the south wall had reached

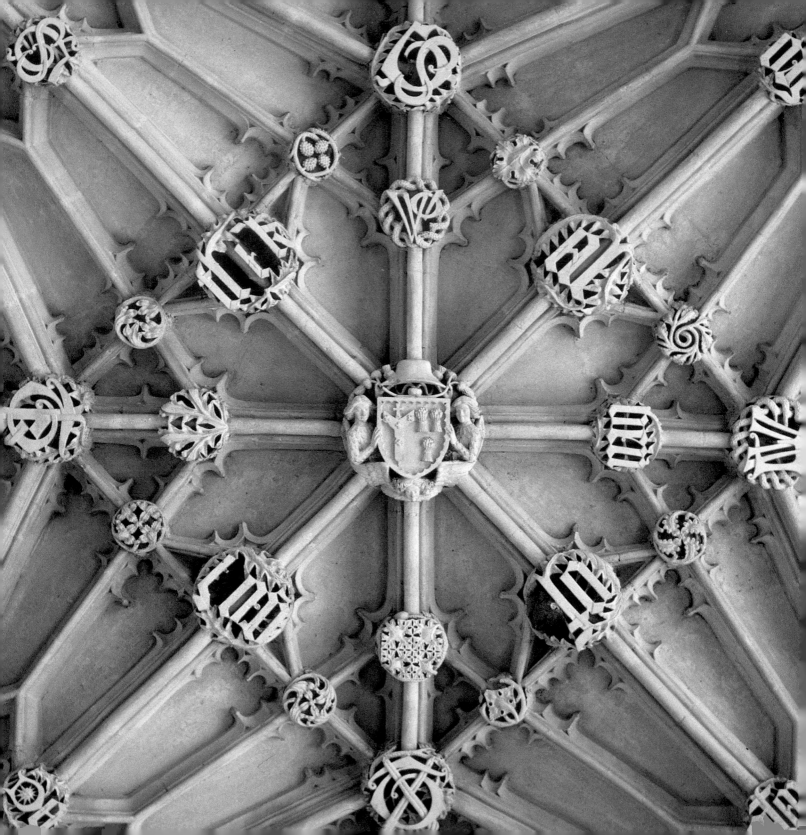

window level, and when the next mason, Thomas Elkyn, took over in 1440 he was told to abandon the elaborate mouldings to the arches, along with 'housings of images, casements and fillets, and other frivolous and irrelevant elaborations' which had been a feature of Winchcombe's work; the effect of this decree can be seen in the lower part of the jambs of the window immediately to the left of the entrance (the easternmost one on the south side).

Elkyn seems to have completed the south wall, but in 1444 the design of the building was modified in an even more fundamental manner when the university decided to place the books donated by Humfrey, Duke of Gloucester, in a new room above the School. Two more masons, Robert Janyns and John Atkyns, started work on this project in 1452–3, but the funding again dried up and the Divinity School was not ready for use until 1470. Even then it lacked the stone vault which is now its chief glory. This was the result of a final building campaign carried out in response to begging letters from the University. The money was available by 1478, when a local master-mason, William Orchard, was brought in to supervise the work. The decision to construct a vault, albeit of lower pitch than that intended fifty years before, necessitated raising the floor-level of the library and also the height of the library windows and walls. Work was finally finished by 1488, when the library was at last opened.

The immediate impression on entering the Divinity School is of light, space and intricately carved stonework encrusting the ceiling, with large pendants hanging from the pointed arches which span the building and hold up

Detail of the ceiling of the Divinity School (left). The Wren Door (right).

the vault. Clusters of ribs sprout, as it were, from the pendants, linked by shorter ribs (liernes), with carved stone bosses at the intersections. These bosses, 455 in number, are carved for the most part with inscriptions and with the coats of arms and initials of donors, including 'WO' for the mason William Orchard; the three wheatsheaves which constitute the arms of Thomas Kemp, Bishop of London and the main donor, can be seen at the centre of the easternmost bay, immediately on entering, and the royal coat of arms is in a comparable position in the third bay, halfway down the building. Among the religious emblems are representations of the Virgin and Child (northern portion of the third bay, over the doorway) and the Trinity (in a comparable position on the south side). There are also lively figures of people and animals, including an eagle and child (east bay), a fox carrying off a goose (in the second bay from the east) and a man picking grapes (third bay). The small figures in the pendants include representations of the four Evangelists and the four Doctors of the Church, and there are figures of the Virgin Mary, St Peter, St Paul and St John on the east wall and of the Virgin and Child over the west door; figures of bishops, angels and seraphim are carved in the jambs of the outer arches on the east and west walls.

The Divinity School has undergone several alterations since the fifteenth century. The stained glass in the windows was smashed after the Reformation, and when the Convocation House was built against the west end in 1634 the spiral staircases leading upstairs to Duke Humfrey's Library were removed. Further changes took place in 1669 under the direction of Christopher Wren, designer of the Sheldonian Theatre, whose show front

can be seen through the windows on the north side. The Theatre was built as a setting for University ceremonial, and in order to allow processions to pass easily to it from the Divinity School – where robes were donned, as they still are on degree days – a doorway was built in 1669 in the north wall, with a pointed arch and the letters C.W.A. (Christopher Wren, architect). Wren also installed iron cramps, which still survive, on the transverse arches, to prevent them being pushed apart by the weight of the books in the library above; further repairs to the vault were carried out in 1700 and again in the twentieth century.

The alterations of 1669 included the installation of new wooden fittings at the west end. Until the nineteenth century degrees were given by disputation, with the candidate giving oral replies to questions posed by an interlocutor, each of them occupying a pulpit on either side of the room; the moderator occupied a higher pulpit between the two. The two lower pulpits still survive, though reduced in height, but the professor's pulpit, which stood in front of the doorway into the Convocation House, has been removed to the Examination Schools. Three valuable pieces of furniture are preserved at the east end of the room: Sir Thomas Bodley's chest, painted with his coat of arms and that of the University, and used for storing money and valuables until 1774; a 'mathematical chest' with four locks, given by Sir Henry Savile and used to protect the funds supporting the professorships of Geometry and Astronomy, both established by him; and a chair made up of timber from Sir Francis Drake's ship the Golden Hind, in which he circumnavigated the globe.

The Convocation House

The Convocation House comprises most of the ground floor of the wing built at right angles onto the west end of the Divinity School in 1634–7. It was built as the meeting place for the University's supreme legislative body, made up of all Masters of Arts who had kept their names on the books of their colleges. Convocation had existed since the thirteenth century, and it recovered some of its lost powers under statutes passed at the instigation of the Chancellor, Archbishop Laud, in 1636. In the nineteenth century most of its powers passed to Congregation – made up of resident Masters of Arts who held teaching or administrative posts in the University, or college fellowships – and today Convocation only functions when a new Chancellor of the University or a Professor of Poetry has to be elected, the elections taking place in the Convocation House.

Convocation House (right). Detail of the seating (below).

The room is lit by large traceried Gothic windows whose archaic style belies their date. The wooden seating is arranged around all four sides, with the Vice-Chancellor's throne, under a domed canopy, at the south end. The wood panelling, which extends halfway up the walls, is richly embellished in the manner of several of the college chapels of the same date, with a repetitious pattern of perspective arches separated from each other by Ionic pilasters. The original ceiling was of plaster, but in 1758–9 the local master-mason John Townesend replaced it with a stone fan vault, an extraordinary and, for its date, almost unique exercise in medieval building techniques which could easily have been built 300 years earlier. The doorway at the northern end of the room leads into the Chancellor's Court (formerly known as the Apodyterium), a smaller square room with another fan vault and more panelling of the 1630s.

The Convocation House housed Charles I's Parliament while the King was resident in Oxford during the Civil War, from 1642–6. The House of Commons met there twice during the reign of his son Charles II: in 1665, when London was stricken by the Plague, and in 1681, when the King chose to hold a session in Oxford in order to exert pressure on members who were attempting to exclude his younger brother (later James II) from the succession. Since then the room has been little used except for University business, and its furnishings have remained virtually unaltered.

Arts End

Until the 1630s, Duke Humfrey's Library was reached by spiral staircases in turrets at the western corners of the Divinity School, but since then it has been approached from staircases in the projections at the south-west and north-west corners of the Schools Quadrangle; these were first built in 1613–19 to give access to the Schools of Law and Medicine in the north and south ranges, and to the second-floor gallery. The present staircases – of wood and with twisted balusters – replaced those of 1613–19 in the mid-seventeenth century. From them the stone carving on the front of the 1610–12 façade of the library can be clearly seen, and near the top of the southern staircase, usually used by visitors, is a marble tablet recording major benefactions to the library.

The staircases lead into Arts End, a long, light room of 1610–12 with a timber tie-beam roof painted with 'grotesques' (fanciful curvaceous designs, popular in the Italian Renaissance, incorporating representations of animals and human heads); the panels contain the University's coat of arms, with Sir Thomas Bodley's arms placed at the intersections of the beams. The cornice moulding is interspersed with grotesque heads, some of them retaining their original colouring. Over the archway into Duke Humfrey's Library are the insignia of the Tudor monarchy. The bookcases extend the full height of the walls: a novelty in early seventeenth-century England, though not on the Continent. The three lower shelves originally contained chained folio books, which were read at the desks in front of them; the chains were removed in the eighteenth century. Smaller books were shelved above, both below and above the wooden gallery, to which there was restricted access; some are still shelved in the normal pre-nineteenth-century manner, with the spines facing inwards. Some panels of seventeenth-century Dutch or Flemish glass, originally at Wytham Abbey, just outside Oxford, have been placed in the south window, and in the top light of the east window, facing the Tower of the Orders on the opposite side of the quadrangle, is a painted-glass representation of the arms of the University, dating from c.1710.

Arts End (left). Detail of ceiling in Arts End (above).

Duke Humfrey's Library and Selden End

Duke Humfrey's Library is entered through a rounded arch, on either side of which are busts of Sir Thomas Bodley, given by Thomas Sackville, Earl of Dorset, Chancellor of the University, in 1605 (left), and of Charles I (right), given by Archbishop Laud in 1636. Bodley's bust was 'carved to the life by an excellent hand at London' (who remains unidentified), and retains its original colouring; the bust of Laud, by Hubert le Sueur, is of bronze, and its elaborate plaster surround of 1641 is by John Jackson, who later designed and built the library and chapel of Brasenose College. The bookcases were all introduced by Bodley when he remodelled the 'great desolate room' in 1598–1602, but the basic structure of the fifteenth-century library survives, with its much-renewed tie-beam roof trusses resting on carved corbels, and its small Perpendicular Gothic windows, with carved

Fifteenth-century stained glass of St Thomas Becket at the court of the King of France and of King Henry II at Becket's shrine (above). Bookcases in Duke Humfrey's Library (right).

head-stops below the arches, lighting the reading spaces between the bookcases. The cases stand on the sites of the original lecterns, under which the chained books were stored (the readers stood up to read them). The main embellishment is on the ceiling, with Renaissance-inspired arabesque designs painted on the beams, and panels of the University's coat of arms – more repetitious than those in Arts End – on the ceiling panels. The walls above the bookcases are lined with portraits, some of them fanciful, of the founders of the colleges.

The library originally contained books connected with the 'higher faculties' (theology, law and medicine) and shelved according to these divisions; everything else came under the heading of 'Arts' and was placed in Arts End. The accumulation of new books made it necessary to construct wooden galleries over the cases in 1693 but they were removed in 1877.

At the far (west) end is Selden End (not open to the public), reached through a rounded arch surmounted by a wooden pediment. Built in 1632–7, though not completed internally until 1640, it is placed above the Convocation House, giving the whole complex – Selden End, Duke Humfrey's Library and Arts End – the shape of a letter H, as Sir Thomas Bodley had intended. Selden End is similar in dimensions to Arts End and is also lit by large Gothic windows, now containing panels of fifteenth-century stained glass (west) and later painted glass (north and south). Some of the glass, including the

Detail of Duke Humfrey's Library (left). Founders and benefactors of the old colleges as depicted in the early seventeenth century, from Duke Humfrey's Library (right).

superb fifteenth-century English panels of St Thomas
Becket at the court of the King of France and of King
Henry II at Becket's shrine, at the bottom of the west
window, was donated by a well-known local antiquary,
Alderman William Fletcher, in 1797; most of the painted
glass, of Flemish origin, comes from later donations,
notably by Denis King, who rearranged the glass
throughout the Library in 1964–9.

The books are stacked on shelves against the walls,
with the upper shelves reached from galleries of rather
more solid-looking wooden construction than those
in Arts End; the original locked cases for valuable
manuscripts still survive, with their ornamented grilles.
There is a flat wooden ceiling, ornamented with painted
heraldry. The room originally housed John Selden's
books and other special collections, as can be seen from
the inscription on the painted cornice. It was occasionally
used for banquets, one of which was attended by King
James II in 1687, watched by eager onlookers who later
consumed the remains of the 111 dishes; it now contains
reference books on topographical and antiquarian
subjects, and on palaeography and codicology.

Selden End (left). Detail of Selden End (right).

The Lower and Upper Reading Rooms

The Lower Reading Room was formed in the 1950s out of the former schools on the first floor of the quadrangle (Law, Languages, Arithmetic and Geometry, Astronomy), which had long been used for storing books and manuscripts. It now houses books on classics and theology.

The top floor of the quadrangle was originally used partly as a book store and partly as a museum and gallery, which was open to the public. The gallery was housed mainly in the south range, and was gradually filled with pictures, coins and other artefacts donated to the University; they are now dispersed throughout several university buildings, but many of the portraits remain in different parts of the library. The painted

frieze, dating from c.1616–19, is adorned with 200 imaginary portraits of writers whose works were and are in the library. They were chosen by the first Librarian, Thomas James, who drew some of his ideas from A. Thevet's *Pourtraits et vies des hommes illustres* (1584). Like the books in the library, the portraits are grouped according to faculty, with the Arts represented in the north range (Homer to Sir Philip Sidney), Medicine and Law in the east range, and Theology in the south range, arranged more or less chronologically from the early Church Fathers to champions of the Reformation in Britain and the Continent. The frieze was covered up when the gallery was restored by Sir Robert Smirke in 1830, and the present wooden ceiling

dates from then, replacing an earlier one with painted
panels, some of which survive above the bookcases
in the south range. Parts of the gallery were turned
into a reading room in 1907 and 1927, the frieze was
uncovered and restored in 1949, and the present
reading room, housing collections to support research
in history and English literature, was created in 1955.
The panels of Flemish painted glass were placed in their
present positions in 1964–9.

Seventeenth-century painted frieze of writers in the Upper Reading
Room (above), the restoration of which is commemorated in a new
frieze section (below).

The Radcliffe Camera

The Radcliffe Library (or Radcliffe Camera, as it has been called since the 1860s) originated with a bequest of £40,000 by Dr John Radcliffe for the building of a new library to be situated close to the Bodleian. He died in 1714, and in the following year the first moves were taken towards acquiring a site to the south of the Schools Quadrangle, between Catte Street and School Street; an earlier scheme, conceived shortly before Radcliffe's death, to build the library against the west end of Selden End foundered because of the excessive compensation demanded by the Fellows of Exeter College, into whose garden the new building would have encroached.

The Trustees of the bequest resolved in 1720 to ask seven of the 'ablest architects' for designs, but of those named only one, Nicholas Hawksmoor, is known to have supplied designs. A pupil of Sir Christopher Wren, he had already designed the Clarendon Building (see below) to the north of the Schools, and had prepared designs in about 1712–3 for remodelling the central academic area of Oxford in a more monumental classical manner, including the creation of an open space or 'Forum Universitatis' on the site of Radcliffe Square. He made several designs for the Radcliffe Library next to Selden End, and in 1715 he prepared a further scheme for one attached to the south wall of the Schools Quadrangle. Most of his designs were for a circular building, inspired

Interior of the dome of the Radcliffe Camera.

perhaps by Wren's earlier, unexecuted design for a circular library at Trinity College, Cambridge. Circular domed buildings conjured up images of Roman mausolea, and Thomas Salmon, in his *The Present State of the Universities* (1744), wrote that 'whatever the Doctor designed or expected from his laying out of £40,000 in building one room, I find a great many People of opinion that he intended to perpetuate his memory by it, and therefore give it the name of Ratcliff's Mausoleum': an idea borne out by the diarist Thomas Hearne, who said that Radcliffe was 'very ambitious of glory'.

Building could not start until after the death of Radcliffe's two sisters, the second of whom died in 1736, but the demolition of the houses in Catte Street and School Street started in 1733. A year later, in 1734, the Trustees called upon Hawksmoor and James Gibbs, another of the architects mentioned in 1720, to submit more detailed designs. Hawksmoor proposed a domed circular library on a square base, rather more austere in its external treatment than his proposal of 1715. Gibbs, on the other hand, sent in designs for a rectangular building in a restrained and dignified classical style, which would have taken up most of the space between the Schools Quadrangle and the University Church of St Mary the Virgin. It seems that Hawksmoor's design won the favour of the Trustees, and he went on to prepare a model, which still survives in the Bodleian. But he died in 1736, and the commission reverted to Gibbs, the architect of the present building.

James Gibbs, architect of the Radcliffe Camera (above left). Dr John Radcliffe (below left). Interior of the Upper Camera (right).

James Gibbs was a rarity among British architects in having been trained in Rome, under Carlo Fontana, a pupil of Gianlorenzo Bernini. He returned to England in 1709 and built up a substantial public and private practice, numbering among his patrons several Tory aristocrats, including one of the Radcliffe Trustees,

the 2nd Earl of Lichfield, whose house at Ditchley, a few miles north of Oxford, was built to his designs in 1720–42. Oxford under the early Hanoverian kings was a hotbed of Toryism, and the employment of Gibbs must have been welcome on political as well as aesthetic grounds. But, perhaps at the instigation of the Trustees, he abandoned his scheme for a rectangular building, and opted for a circular plan, with a dome which has, ever since its construction, been one of the main landmarks of Oxford. The foundation stone was laid in 1737, and building was finished in 1748.

The library stands in the middle of Radcliffe Square, further from the Schools Quadrangle than had originally been intended. It was built of local limestone, with 'hardstone' from the nearby quarries at Headington for the ground floor, and ochre-coloured stone from Burford, some 20 miles away, for the upper floor (since refaced). The architectural effect is both rich and subtle, revealing something of Gibbs's early exposure to the Roman Baroque. The ground floor is rusticated, and was originally a public open space entered through large archways under pediments, with gates which were closed at night; the bays between the arches are occupied by niches (which never held statues). The main reading room is upstairs, and is ringed externally by pairs of engaged Corinthian columns, with two windows in each alternate bay; the other, narrower, bays, which are part of the buttressing system for the dome, have blind niches. Above the cornice and balustrade, interrupted by

Staircase of Radcliffe Camera (left). The Lower Camera (overleaf).

urns, rises the dome on its drum, pierced with windows lighting the central rotunda. Gibbs originally planned to construct the dome of stone, and stone buttresses were built for this purpose, but in the end it was decided to build it of timber, with a lead covering. The lines of the buttresses are continued upwards as ribs on the surface of the dome, and at the top there is a domed lantern.

The building is entered from the south, and an internal spiral staircase mounts up to the first floor from the far end; an outer staircase on the north side, added in 1862, is no longer used. The internal staircase is of stone, and is cantilevered out from the walls; the balustrade is of iron and the domed ceiling is covered with plasterwork of Rococo inspiration, by one or more of the three plasterers employed on the building: Joseph Artari, a Swiss-Italian who often worked on Gibbs's buildings, Charles Stanley, born in Denmark, and the Oxford-born Thomas Roberts. At the top of the stairs are a bust of James Gibbs and portraits of John Radcliffe and Francis Smith of Warwick, one of the two builders employed to construct the building to Gibbs's designs, the other one being William Townesend, the leading Oxford master-builder of the time; both men died soon after building began, and were succeeded by their sons.

The interior of the main reading room survives much as Gibbs and his team of craftsmen left it, save for the introduction of desks into the central rotunda and the covering of the black and white marble floor. The main doorway is surmounted by a posthumous life-size statue of Dr Radcliffe by John Michael Rysbrack, carved in 1744–7 and enclosed within a pedimented niche. The central space is surrounded by an arcade of round arches resting on massive stone piers articulated by pairs of Ionic pilasters. There are exuberantly carved stone cartouches in the spandrels of the arches, and above them is a bold cornice. The arcade supports the drum of the dome, above which is the inner shell of the dome itself, richly decorated in plaster and restored to the original colour scheme by Robert Potter in 1969. The books – ostensibly the raison d'etre of this massive structure – have always been arranged in cases around the outer walls, behind the arcade. They are placed in two levels, with a gallery, encased by a balustrade, giving access to the upper level. There is some excellent plasterwork on the ceiling of the lower level, beneath the gallery.

For many years the Radcliffe Library attracted few readers, although it was sometimes used on festive occasions, notably a banquet attended by the King of Prussia and the Tsar of Russia in 1814. After being taken over by the Bodleian in 1860 it gradually became a much-frequented reading-room for undergraduates; the ground floor was enclosed and used for the storage of books, but became a second reading room in 1941. The ground floor reading room, part of the History Faculty Library, has a low saucer dome of stone and a Tuscan doorcase on the north side, which originally marked the only entrance to the staircase leading to the main library upstairs; by the doorway is an inscription honouring Lee Seng Tee, a resident of Singapore and Honorary Fellow of Oriel College, who funded the restoration of this part of the building in 1999.

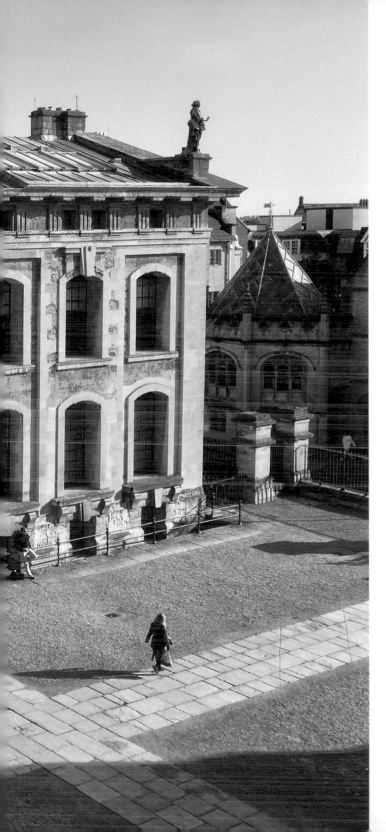

The Clarendon Building

This monumental classical structure was built in 1712–13, to the designs of Nicholas Hawksmoor, as the headquarters and printing-works of the Oxford University Press, which had until then been housed in the Sheldonian Theatre; much of the funding came from the profits of Lord Clarendon's *History of the Great Rebellion* (1702–4).

The building occupies a site just to the north of the old city wall, the line of which can be traced in the paving between it and the Schools Quadrangle, one of Oxford's most impressive architectural spaces. The Sheldonian Theatre is on the west side of the site, and the open east side looks out to Hertford College, with T.G. Jackson's so-called 'Bridge of Sighs' (1913–14) spanning New College Lane, and the late-fourteenth-century tower of New College. An opening between the Sheldonian Theatre and the Schools Quadrangle leads into a smaller courtyard from which the outside of the Divinity School and Duke Humfrey's Library can be seen.

Hawksmoor saw the Clarendon Building as an impressive ceremonial entrance to the central University area. The northern approach, from Broad Street, leads up a flight of steps through a massive Doric portico and into a passageway which bisects the building and is aligned with the archways leading into the Schools Quadrangle from the north and south; the portico is echoed on the south front, facing the Schools

The south elevation of the Clarendon Building.

Quadrangle, and the walls are treated in a highly sculptural manner, with heavily emphasized keystones and window architraves.

A Doric frieze runs around the building at eaves level, and the east and west gable-ends both take the form of pediments, giving the sense of two intersecting classical temples. A figure by Francis Bird of the Earl of Clarendon, one of the leading politicians of the early years of Charles II's reign, occupies a niche on the upper floor of the western side of the building, facing the Sheldonian Theatre, and lead figures of the Muses by Sir James Thornhill enliven the roofline. The building was originally divided between the Learned Press, and the Bible Press, separated by the passageway. The most impressive of the interiors is the Delegates' Room (not open to the public), beautifully panelled in oak with Corinthian pilasters and a portrait of Queen Anne over the fireplace. The Press moved out in 1830, after the construction of the present premises in Walton Street, and for many years afterwards the building was used for University administrative business, latterly housing the Registry.

In 1975 it was taken over by the Bodleian as administrative offices, though a robing-room for the Vice-Chancellor is retained, furnished with Napoleonic items bequeathed by Lord Curzon of Kedleston, Chancellor from 1907 to 1925.

Two of the eight muses on the roofline of the Clarendon Building.

The New Library

By the 1920s the library buildings were full to capacity, and in 1931 it was decided to build a major extension. Proposals to build an entirely new library half a mile away in the University Parks having been turned down, a site was chosen on the north side of Broad Street, facing the Clarendon Building. Much of the funding came from the Rockefeller Foundation – one of the first of many instances of American generosity to Oxford University – and in 1934 Sir Giles Gilbert Scott, designer of the Cambridge University Library, the Anglican cathedral at Liverpool and the celebrated red telephone box, was chosen as architect; the building went up in 1937–40.

The New Bodleian was essentially a huge warehouse or storage facility for some five million books, enfolded by offices and reading rooms, and rising to a taller stack tower, the latter all but invisible from the street; the design owed much to recent American precedent, notably the Sterling Library at Yale University, which Scott had visited. A group of seventeenth- and eighteenth-century houses was demolished to make way for the new building, which was set back from the line of Broad Street, creating a potentially attractive open space, which has been enhanced in the recent (2014) remodelling. The core of the new building was occupied by a steel-framed book stack, eleven storeys high and partially sunk into the ground so as to reduce the height; it was closed to readers, the books being transported to the reading rooms in the existing library by a conveyor belt through an underground tunnel. Scott did his best

to impart some architectural interest to the elevations, but his efforts pleased few of the critics, especially when compared to those of Nicholas Hawksmoor in the Clarendon Building opposite, and the bulky, fortress-like exterior remained little-admired. The outside walls are of rubble stone from Bladon, a few miles north of Oxford - a favourite building material in inter-war Oxford – with Clipsham stone dressings; one eminent architectural historian compared the effect to that of a dinner jacket made of Harris Tweed. The detailing is loosely classical; the ornament, wrote Scott, was 'only used where it serves a definite aesthetic purpose, and not applied inordinately merely to enrich the building.' A bust of Sir Thomas Bodley occupies a niche breaking through the rounded pediment over the rarely-used ceremonial entrance from Broad Street, placed carefully so as to establish a visual link through the Clarendon Building and the Schools Quadrangle to the Radcliffe Camera: something that can still be enjoyed. But when the building was formally opened by King George VI in 1946 the key broke in the lock.

By the beginning of the twenty-first century the New Bodleian had become full to overflowing, and a decision was taken to build a capacious new book storage facility away from the main library site. A new warehouse for eight and a half million books, with 153 miles of shelving, was opened in 2010 on the outskirts of Swindon, thirty miles away; from here books are brought by road to the Oxford reading rooms. A further change occurred

in 2011 when, as part of a major reconfiguration of the Library's collections and reading rooms, an underground bookstore beneath the Radcliffe Camera was opened to readers, allowing them open access to recently-published books; it is linked by a tunnel (the Gladstone Link) to the Old Library.

In 2006 the firm of Wilkinson Eyre Architects was commissioned to remodel the New Bodleian as a Special Collections research library, together with seminar rooms, conservation studios and public exhibition galleries. Completed in 2014, the Weston Library, as it is now known, retains as much as possible of Scott's structure, while opening up the building to readers and visitors, and supplying up-to-date protection for the Bodleian's priceless collections of books and manuscripts. The staircase from Broad Street, replacing a former inaccessible plinth, leads to an entrance colonnade beyond which is a spacious top-lit entrance hall, created by removing the central book stack. From here visitors are able to reach the two exhibition galleries, one displaying material from the permanent collection, the other for special exhibitions, and a lecture room. To the left are a café and shop, and to the right the readers' entrance, enclosed within a late-sixteenth-century gate surround from Ascott Park, near Stadhampton, Oxfordshire, rescued from the storerooms of the Victoria and Albert Museum.

The New Library shortly after construction.

The two main reading rooms – formerly the reading rooms for Politics, Philosophy and Economics and a catalogue room - are on the first floor, and are reached by Scott's main staircase on the eastern side of the building; they are decorated in a restrained Art Deco manner found throughout the public areas of the original building. From here, readers have access to a gallery overlooking the atrium-like entrance hall. Another reading room occupies the top floor of Scott's stack tower, lit by his characteristic tall, thin slit-like windows; it commands rooftop views over Broad Street to the Clarendon Building, Sheldonian Theatre and Old Library. The middle floor of the new upper stack also contains the Centre for the Study of the Book, a research centre with offices for visiting scholars and a common room. Closed stack books are stored in a basement stack underneath the entrance hall, and open access books in a high-level 'floating stack' supported by two concrete 'cores' containing lifts and services.

Scott's New Bodleian was originally expected to serve the library's needs for 200 years, but in 1937 he asked whether 'libraries, as we know them will by then have ceased to exist, and a central television station will send wireless visions of books to readers' homes and they will turn the pages by pressing a button!' The architect's vision of the technological future has come to pass earlier than he anticipated. But libraries have not been made redundant, and the new Weston Library is a triumphant expression of confidence in their future.

Further Reading

G. Barber, *Arks for Learning* (1995)
M. Clapinson, *A Brief History of the Bodleian Library* (2014)
E. Craster, *History of the Bodleian Library 1845–1945* (1952)
S. Gillam, *The Divinity School and Duke Humfrey's Library at Oxford* (1988, revised 1998)
S. Gillam, *The Radcliffe Camera* (1992)
D. Rogers, *The Bodleian Library and its Treasures* (1991)
I. Philip, *The Bodleian Library in the Seventeenth and Eighteenth Centuries* (1983)
S. Hebron, *Marks of Genius* (2015),
S. Hebron, *Dr Radcliffe's Library* (2014),
D. Vaisey, *Bodleian Library Treasures* (2015)

First published in 2000 by the Bodleian Library
Broad Street, Oxford, OX1 3BG, www.bodleianshop.co.uk
This revised edition published in 2014

ISBN: 978 1 85124 274 0

Cover design by Dot Little at the Bodleian Library
Designed and typeset by Bonnie Bryan and Dot little in 10/14pt Gill Sans
Printed and bound by Grafos SA, Barcelona, on 135gsm Magnosatin paper

Author's note
In quoting from old letters and documents I have modernized the spelling. I am grateful to Geoff Turner of Wilkinson Eyre Architects for his assistance with information about the Weston Library.

Photography Credits
© John Downing, p. 38; © Ahmet Ertug, pp. 4–5; Fetherstonhaugh Associates, p. 35; © Darrell Godliman, front cover; Ian Jackson, pp. 23, 24, 27, 30, 31, 33, 39, back cover; © Fr Lawrence Lew, O.P., pp. 18, 20; © Greg Smolonski, inside front and back cover, 2–3, 11, 16, 19, 22, 32, 34, 36, 40–41, 42–43, 44, 45, 46, 48–49, 49–50, 52.